REBOUND, RETURN, RESTORE

Jeremiah Sinsheimer

ISBN 978-1-0980-8809-5 (paperback)
ISBN 978-1-0980-8810-1 (digital)

Christian Faith Publishing, Inc.
832 Park Avenue
Meadville, PA 16335
www.christianfaithpublishing.com

Printed in the United States of America

CONTENTS

Acknowledgments

I WOULD LIKE TO THANK my wonderful wife, Svetlana, without whom, I would never have become all that God intended for me to be. You are the wind beneath my wings. And to our beautiful children—David, Esther, Ruth, Isaiah, and Abigail—for supporting me in the writing of this book, I say thank you! Without your love and support, this would not have been possible. I love you all!

Also, I would like to thank my parents for giving me Jesus and showing me the love of God. You have given to me the most important thing a parent can give their child: a foundation on Christ.

A special thank-you to Nick Gromiko for a wonderful book title that truly explains what is written within this book.

Thank you to my friend Gevork Manucharian and his family for supporting me in the production of this book. God bless you!

Thank you to our wonderful church family, Good News Christian Church, for all your prayers and support. It is a privilege to be your pastor. Most importantly, thank you, Lord Jesus, for your wonderful love and revealing yourself to me through your word. I love you, Lord!

INTRODUCTION

IN MY MANY YEARS OF serving the Lord, I never understood fully just how much His Spirit beckoned me to come up to a higher place where I could dwell with Him for eternity, a place called the House of Bread. Although many people feel like the House of Bread is the House of Death, I hope that you will be changed by reading this book. You will see that God is faithful and that His house is a House of Bread and Life.

My prayer is that as you read this book, you would also desire to come to the place known as the House of Bread. Many people desire God to move where they're standing when God calls them to come to where He is at the House of Bread.

May your desire to read this book compel you to know Him more and be in His presence. My hope and prayer is that you find His life in the House of Bread and that you would receive a refreshed call on your life to live for Him and find Him in everything and in every situation. May God bless you as you read this book, and may He reveal Himself to you.

1

THE HOUSE OF BREAD

WHAT I WOULD LIKE TO share with you is a very important topic that really touches every believer who feel burned out at times or feel like somehow God has forsaken them or has been unfaithful to them while they served Him.

In the book of Ruth, we see that there was once a family living in Bethlehem who lost everything they had due to the fact that they lived in unbelief. Their names were Elimilech, Naomi, Mahlon, and Chilion. This family lived during the times when the judges ruled Israel. They lived in the town of Bethlehem.

> *In the days when the judges ruled in Israel, a severe famine came upon the land. So a man from Bethlehem in Judah left his home and went to live in the country of Moab, taking his wife and two sons with him.* (Ruth 1:1)

Now the Bible says that in those days, there was a famine in Bethlehem. This, in and of itself, is bewildering to me because the Jewish word for house is *beit*, and the Jewish word for bread is *lehem*.

So how can you say that there is a famine in the house of bread? That just doesn't make any sense, does it? A famine in a place of abundance, famine in a place known for its bread, how does that happen? How does a place known for feeding people become a place of starvation? Most importantly, where were the judges? What were they doing during a time of famine? Were they feeding themselves? Were they ignoring the needs of the people? Most importantly, what brought Bethlehem to this place?

First, let's take a closer look at the city of Bethlehem. It was once known for its abundance. Although Bethlehem is the smallest city in Israel, it is one of the most legendary because of its important role in history as well as in Jewish prophesy. In history, when a city was named, it was named by what it was known for. For instance, in our time the city of Las Vegas is better known as Sin City. Why? Because of its sinful atmosphere. The same is said for Bethlehem. It was once known for being a little city that makes good bread. A *house of bread.*

So at what point did the house of bread not produce bread? I believe that it did not happen overnight or suddenly. It was a slow process in which people grew accustomed to less and less bread, until they suddenly realized that they were starving. By that point, they needed divine intervention to feed them again. They came to a crossroads in their lives so that they had to call upon the Lord. They soon had such a hunger for bread that they couldn't take starving anymore.

Have you ever found yourself in that place spiritually? I believe this is an example of the church in modern times. The church of Jesus Christ is supposed to be known for its life-giving bread that feeds the entire world. It is the modern-day house of bread, the place where people can come to eat the living manna from heaven and be filled in their souls. Somehow though, the church itself is in a state of complete starvation.

That is an oxymoron to me. How does the modern-day house of bread fall into a place of total starvation that not only can they not feed others, they can't even feed themselves? How does the manna cease to exist in a place that is supposed to be producing bread? Why does this happen in a place that should never experience starvation? Has God given up on His church? Absolutely not! He said in Joshua chapter 1 verse 5 that He would never leave us nor forsake us. If we are feeling like God is not near, then maybe we need to take a better look at ourselves and see what is hindering His presence from being close to us. Perhaps God hasn't forsaken us, but we have forsaken Him.

You see, for Bethlehem, they allowed things that hindered the production of bread and caused them to experience starvation. God didn't stop blessing Israel and Bethlehem, but they did something that stopped the flow of God's blessing in their lives.

People think that whenever Israel sinned against God, He would punish them constantly. We have this misconception of who God is and how He responds to our mistakes. We think that God is just waiting for us to mess up, that somehow He takes pleasure in seeing us come up short of what He wants us to become. This is the worst idea of God's character among many Christians. More often than not, the things that we go through in our lives are a direct result of our own poor decisions, resulting in consequences that are negative. I'm not saying that God doesn't punish sin because He has to punish sin. However, He doesn't look to punish the sinner unless that person is living in absolute rebellion against His laws.

For the Christian, however, if he is experiencing death or starvation in his spiritual walk, that could be nothing more than him allowing other things between his relationship with Jesus Christ and, as a result, he is not getting the living bread from heaven. Now the bottom line is, are you hindering your own self from eating the living bread or is Jesus Christ a lair? Because He said:

> *I am the living bread which comes down*
> *from heaven. If anyone eats of this bread, he*
> *will live forever.* (John 6:51)

So now we should ask ourselves this question, Am I eating this bread or have I allowed other things in my mouth so that I cannot eat that which will give me true life?

For Bethlehem, they might have decided to export more bread than they could produce, resulting in not enough products needed for their own survival. Maybe there was a shortage of laborers in the fields not producing enough wheat for flour to make bread for Israel. Whatever may have happened to put Israel and Bethlehem in that position, it had dire consequences, resulting in panic and worry. The citizens of Israel were perhaps forced to reexamine themselves to see why this famine started in the first place.

Maybe the Israelites started looking at their own hearts and lives to see where they messed up so that they could return to a right relationship with God and once again prosper, particularly Bethlehem. The house of bread needed to start producing bread again to feed Israel, but first the house of bread needed to do some house cleaning before it could get back to being the house with the reputation of producing bread. I believe that that is exactly what started happening. People began looking at their leaders. The judges started examining how they were being lead and what they needed to do differently.

If you want to live spiritually and eat of the "bread of life," then you need to see what other things have gotten in the way. What or who has become more valuable to you than Jesus Christ? You may have certain idols in your life that is robbing you of your time with God. Perhaps you go to church not for spiritual growth, but social fellowship. Maybe you, as God's church, stopped producing bread and started producing something sweeter like cake. You decided that somewhere along the way you would do things your way and create compromises in your walk, not realizing that the more you compromised, the less bread you ate, the more you starved spiritually. It is possible that other people have influenced you in such a way that you no longer have the reputation of being a house of bread as the church, but rather an old flour mill that has stopped producing bread and feeding people by your testimony. Whatever the case might be, you know that you are starving and you long for the power and presence of God.

However, many of us know that when things get tough, some people look at themselves and correct what is wrong in their own lives, while others look to another place to find life and satisfaction in spite of what those around them are doing.

This was the case for a man named Elimelech, his wife Naomi, and their sons. Elimelech decided that he could no longer live in the house of bread during a time of famine, so he took the easy way out and headed for Moab. He thought that the problem was with the place he lived and not with him. He saw that while God's people suffered in Bethlehem, the heathen were getting all the good stuff in life. He was overcome by his own lusts and desires for the easy life and the easy road that he didn't take time to examine himself to see if maybe he needed to change. He took his wife and sons to a place I like to call the house of death.

This problem with Elimelech started way before he decided to leave Bethlehem. It started while he was living for years in the house of bread. Elimelech created within his own household a negative atmosphere. Even though his name means "my God is King," he didn't live in that faith the way that his parents intended for him to when they gave him the name. He was from the tribe of Ephraim. This tribe was blessed by God through Jacob. The name Ephraim means *fruitful*. Elimelech was called as an Ephrathite to be fruitful where he was. He married a woman named Naomi.

Her name in the Hebrew means *pleasant*, yet we see later in the scriptures that she becomes bitter.

Why is that? What happened to this couple? How did they lose sight of the blessing that God had for them? We see that this family was in the house of bread, living as those who were called to be fruitful, whose God is King, called to be pleasant, and yet they leave this place. This is what happens when a person allows themselves to become influenced by the situations around them rather than continuing to live by faith.

Elimelech created a negative atmosphere around him by giving his sons' names based upon their situations, not based upon what God had called them to be. His firstborn son's name was Mahlon. The name Mahlon means: sickly. The name of his other son was Chilion. His name means: dying, or wasting away. These boys were born a long time before Elimelech decided to leave Bethlehem. They were young adults by the time they arrived in Moab because they only lived in Moab for ten years before they both died.

At the time of their birth, on the eighth day of their lives, according to the laws of Moses, Elimelech gives them these names. In other words, instead of speaking life into them, instead of speaking blessing into them, and instead of pronouncing God's promises over them, he curses his own sons! He speaks death and destruction over their lives based on his own lack of faith in the power of God. The Bible says that life and death is in the power of the tongue. This is where the negativity started within his home. This happened slowly over a period of many years. This is where Elimelech began to doubt the promises of God in his life and the lives of his family. He allowed the circumstances of that day to dictate the future of his family.

How many of us find ourselves speaking reality over our situations at times rather than clinging to the promises of God in Christ? It is very tempting to do what Elimelech did. We all have the same tendencies. We all find ourselves in places of doubt at times when we are in a situation that is too much for us to handle. So the question becomes: how can I avoid becoming like Elimelech? How do I cling to the promises of God rather than allowing my situations in life to dictate my faith?

Well, we have to go to the scriptures to remember God's promises to us:

> *It is the Lord who goes before you. He will be with you; he will not leave you or forsake you. Do not fear or be dismayed.* (Deuteronomy 31:8)

It's very important that we speak the word of God over our lives. It's important for us to remember what God says about us rather that what our circumstances tell us about ourselves. The more you quote the scripture, the more you allow the Spirit of God to speak that scripture into you and the more you begin to believe in His promises rather than your problems.

God said that He will fight for us. All we have to do is ask Him. We have to make a conscious decision to walk daily in the promises of God. I know that it is difficult to do at times, but if we don't do that, then we will become like Elimelech, and the situations surrounding our lives will turn us negative and unbelieving.

2

THE HOUSE OF DEATH

The man's name was Elimelech, his wife's name was Naomi, and the names of his two sons were Mahlon and Chilion. They were Ephrathites from Bethlehem in Judah, and they entered the land of Moab and settled there.
—Ruth 1:2

ELIMILECH FAILED TO USE THIS opportunity to cry out to God and seek Him. He moved his family to a place absolutely devoid of God's presence. He took them to a place of spiritual death in their lives and really didn't recognize it. You see, when faced with a tough moment in his life, Elimilech chose to run from God rather than run to Him. Instead of asking the Lord to guide him into what he should do, he took matters into his own hands.

How many of us believers have a tendency to run away from the Lord when faced with hardships in life or try and work everything out in our own strength, not realizing that we need Him to guide us? How many of us make the same mistake that Elimilech made? Why do us Christians try to act independent from Christ?

The biggest mistake that Elimilech made in that moment was not going to Moab, but rather forgetting who he was in the Lord. He lost his identity in the Lord even though he was still in the house of bread. His very name means "God is King." His tribe was blessed by being called fruitful, yet he soon forgot who he was called to be in God. His parents dedicated him to the Lord and blessed his life by calling him Elimilech. He was given a blessing so that he remembered forever that the Lord was with him. The problem is that he didn't believe the blessing he was given by his parents at his dedication. Even sadder is that if he would have remembered his family line, he would have known that he came from the tribe of Ephraim.

Jacob blessed Ephraim. We can find this blessing right before Jacob dies. This is what it says:

> *"God, before whom my fathers Abraham*
> *and Isaac walked, the God who has fed me*
> *all my life long to this day,*
> *The Angel who has redeemed me from*
> *all evil, bless the lads;*
> *Let my name be named upon them, and*
> *the name of my fathers Abraham and Isaac;*
> *And let them grow into a multitude in*
> *the midst of the earth."* (Genesis 48:15–16)

He had the blessing of not only his parents, but likewise the blessing that Jacob gave to Ephraim. But whenever a person forgets where they came from, they will also not know who they are. Elimilech forgot that he was an Ephraimite and that his God is King.

How many of us tend to forget our identity in Jesus Christ? We forget that that we are predestined for the glory of God in Christ Jesus. We focus on other things and the material world, forgetting that our God shall supply all our needs. This is something that we struggle with at times as believers.

We cannot fault Elimelech for his shortcomings because as we begin to see his story unfold, we can easily compare ourselves to him. However, his story was placed in the scriptures so that we could learn from his mistakes and not repeat them. Whenever times get tough in life, we tend to run. Just like Elimelech ran away to find greener pastures, we also tend to want to run from a place where we are forced to trust God for our provisions. This happens when the situations that we are in cause us to forget who we are in Christ.

Just as Elimelech forgot his identity, we also can find ourselves forgetting who we are according to the promises of God. I would like to caution you to never allow yourself to forget who you are in Christ, and what He has called you to be. Because if you allow the situations of life to turn you negative, if you focus on only your circumstances, you will soon forget about your walk with Christ and slowly fall away from grace. You will find yourself gradually becoming less satisfied with bread and more desiring the world.

This is what happened to Elimelech. He found himself wanting to eat the meat of Moab rather than the bread of Bethlehem. He thought that he could find other things and other places that would satisfy him. Yet by choosing to run during a time of famine and not living by faith, he lost his own life as well as the lives of his sons. What a sad state of events. I'm sure that if Elimelech were to do it all over again, he would have chosen to change his mentality and remained in Bethlehem. Elimelech left the house of bread because he wanted to survive but found himself in the house of death in Moab instead. You see, this story was placed in the scriptures for us to realize that there is no life outside of the house of bread.

Bethlehem was a place of provision for Israel, even during a famine. Bethlehem continues to be the place for provision for the world. Thousands of years ago, Bethlehem was given the name house of bread. That was not an accident. It was a type and shadow of what was supposed to take place many years later when a young virgin girl brought forth the *bread of life* in a manger one holy night. That very bread still gives His life to a hungry and famished world.

> *"For the bread of God is he who comes down from heaven and gives life to the world." They said to him, "Sir, give us this bread always."*
>
> *Jesus replied, "I am the bread of life. Whoever comes to me will never be hungry again. Whoever believes in me will never be thirsty."* (John 6:33–35)

How often we tend to forget that our life is found only in Him! How often we forget that if we were ever to leave the place of His provision, we would ultimately die. Even if we are faced with difficulties, He is able to meet our needs. He is ready to stop our hunger. All we have to do is ask Him. Just as the Jews asked Him to give them this bread always, we also must ask Him to give us His bread of life.

If we ever make the fateful decision to leave His place of provision, we will enter into the house of death, just like Elimelech. Moab can never satisfy the hunger within you because the hunger within you is a hunger for the bread of life. God never promised us that there wouldn't be difficult times in life. He never promised us that there won't be situations in life that test our faith. However, He did promise us that if we would chose to partake of His presence, we would never hunger again. This is why He gave His life for us! He asked us to eat of this bread. When Jesus was giving the bread to His disciples at the Last Supper, He told them to eat it. When He told the other seventy disciples that they would have to eat of this bread, they walked away. They didn't like the thought of having to constantly abide in Christ to find life. They didn't want to hear that there was no good thing in them that could feed their souls. They refused to remain in that spiritual Bethlehem.

How about you? Where are you right now? Are you trying to find life outside of the bread of life? If you are outside that life-giving house of bread, perhaps it is time to do something that Elimelech never had the opportunity to do—return to Bethlehem.

Then Jesus said, "Come to me, all of you who are weary and carry heavy burdens, and I will give you rest." (Matthew 11:28)

Jesus gives us a second chance if we are willing to ask.

3

MERCY IN MOAB

*But Elimelech, the husband of Naomi, died, and she
was left with her two sons. These took Moabite wives;
the name of the one was Orpah and the name of the
other Ruth. They lived there about ten years, and
both Mahlon and Chilion died, so that the woman
was left without her two sons and her husband.*

—Ruth 1:3–5

HERE WE SEE THE FRUIT of Elimelech's decision. He died
shortly after arriving in Moab. After he died, his sons married Moabite women. They were there for ten years when
tragedy strikes once more. Now Naomi, Elimelech's wife,
lost both of her sons.

Can you imagine how she must have felt at that time?
She left Bethlehem to make a better life, but she had to
attend three funerals instead. She followed her husband to
Moab. Now the one she followed was dead. As if that was
not bad enough, now she lost both of her sons too! Moab
truly become a house of death! She was now facing loneli-
ness, heartbreak, and pain because there are no longer any
men to care for her. Hunger was now present in her life. Her

two daughters-in-law are all she had left, and one of them eventually left her.

Now Naomi had a decision to make, should she stay in the house of death or return to the house of bread? Can you see what one wrong decision can do? Can you see how Elimelech's negativity, lack of faith, and decision to leave the house of bread led to not only his death but also the death of his sons? It likewise put his wife in a place of hunger, heartache, and bitterness.

Whenever we make certain choices in life, we must keep in mind that they may have a direct impact on those around us. We can clearly see what happened to Elimelech as a direct result of his decision. Now let's take a look at his wife, Naomi.

The woman had been though more than you and I would ever care to go through. She left her Hometown, her country, her relatives, her friends, and her culture. She then, while trying to save her family from famine, moved to a foreign country. Of course, this was not just her doing. This was a decision made by Elimelech. However, she went along with it. Now she was left with literally nothing—no husband, no children, no relatives, no work, no food… nothing.

Looking at this from a purely human perspective, you could understand why she became bitter. Elimelech and Naomi both made a poor decision to leave the house of bread, thinking that by doing so they would escape a famine. At first, Naomi didn't see their decision as the reason why they suffered. Naomi was now at a crossroads in her life. She has the option to either stay in Moab or go back to Bethlehem. She chose to return to Bethlehem.

Sometimes when we are facing hardship we don't see where we were wrong. Our focus becomes on our situations rather than on how we got to this point.

> *Then she arose with her daughters-in-law, that she might return from the country of Moab: for she had heard in the country of Moab that the Lord had visited His people in giving them bread. So she departed from the place where she was, and her two daughters-in-law with her; and they went on the way to return to the land of Judah.* (Ruth 1:6–7)

Here Naomi made the decision to return home, only this time she had two other women willing to go with her. One of the women went with her because she pitied her state, while the other woman went because she truly loved her.

Can you imagine what was going through Naomi's head at that moment? She's probably thinking about all of the loss she experienced in Moab. Yet through all she lost, she obtained two women who also experienced her pain because they were widows too. It was bittersweet.

As she began to contemplate her return to Bethlehem, she understood that they were all women, and it would be very difficult for them to survive. It's not like they can just go down to the nearest field and work or fill out an application at the nearest bakery for work. In those days, it was very difficult for women to survive if they were widows without sons to care for them. So now Naomi had to make another difficult decision. She had to send her daughters-in-law back home to Moab. After all, they still had some relatives there to care for them. Perhaps they might even have another opportunity to get married. They were still young enough.

Naomi was probably thinking, *I need to fight for my own survival alone. I don't want to worry these ladies with my own personal problems. I don't want my fight for survival to become their fight too.* So she tried to convince her daughters-in-law to go back home to Moab. Naomi must have been a very good and loving woman for her daughters-in-law to love her so much that they were willing to move with her to a new land. How many of us can say that we have that good of a relationship with our in-laws? This is, however, the case for Naomi.

Naomi decided to return to the house of bread in the land of Judah. The name Judah means "praise." So to put it in other words, Naomi is returning to the house of bread, which is located in a place of praise. The Bible says that when Judah had twins with Tamar, the child that was able to fight his way out first was named Perez. Perez means "breakthrough!" This is why praise is so important. It leads to breakthrough in the life of a believer. That is why the house of bread was located in a place of praise.

Because God wants us to know that when we make a decision to praise Him in spite of our circumstances, we will find bread to satisfy our hungry souls. How many of us don't feel like worshipping God in those moments?

Naomi more than likely felt this way. She's not really in a place in her life where she felt like praising God. She was a broken woman who had lost everything. Now she heard that the Lord visited His people in the house of bread. Naomi decided that she will return to the place that once fed her. A place of God's provision. A place where she once dwelt. Only this time, she had nothing to offer God. She was empty.

Have you ever found yourself in that place where you return to the Lord empty-handed, a place where you feel like you have nothing to offer God? This was the place she was in. However, if she wanted to get back to a place of abundance, if she wanted to get back to a place of life, if she wanted to get back to a place where she could once again experience joy, and if she wanted to once again dwell in the house of bread, she first had to go through praise. This is the key to experiencing breakthrough! It's a moment when you make a decision to worship God in spite of your situation in spite of your problem. It's a moment when you choose to say, "God, I trust you to take me back to a place that I once knew! A place where I experienced Your presence! A place of the life-giving bread of God!"

Naomi thought that she had to do this alone. She told her daughters-in-law to go back home to Moab.

> *And Naomi said to her two daughters-in-law, "Go return each of you to her mother's house. May the Lord deal kindly with you as*

you have dealt with the dead and with me. May the Lord grant that you may find rest, each in the house of her husband." Then she kissed them, and they lifted up their voices and wept. (Ruth 1:8–9)

Naomi blessed her daughters-in-law and said her good-byes to them. She thought that she would walk alone back to a place of bread and life. What is about to take place is what I refer to in this chapter as mercy in Moab. This is the moment when true relationships are tested and true friendships are made known. What happens next surprised Naomi. The ladies made a case for staying with her and returning together to Bethlehem.

And they lifted up their voices and wept again; and Orpah kissed her mother-in-law, but Ruth clung to her. Then she said, "Behold, your sister-in-law has gone back to her people and her gods; return after your sister-in-law." But Ruth said, "Do not urge me to leave you or turn back from following you; for where you go, I will go, and where you stay, I will stay, Your people shall be my people, and your God, my God." (Ruth 1:14–16)

What a clear picture of the mercy of God! You see, we know that Elimelech and Naomi's decision to leave Bethlehem was a wrong one, but God still made a way out for Naomi. It was through a vessel that she never would have suspected. God used her own daughter-in-law to help her return to the place that she needed to be.

Orpah was the daughter-in-law who loved Naomi but felt more sorry for her. The name Orpah means "gazelle" or "stiff-necked." So even though she loved Naomi to a certain extent, she was too "stiff-necked of a gazelle" to change her way of life that would allow her to live for the benefit of others. She loved Naomi but not to the extent that she was willing to give anything up to help her. She still preferred her life, culture, gods, and comfort in her relative's house. That was more important to her.

Have you ever had people like that in your life, especially when you are going through difficulties? You always considered them close, but the minute that circumstances began to test the relationship, they bailed on you. That is what happened to Naomi with Orpah. Even though Naomi told her to return home, she didn't fight that offer. She didn't cling to her the way that Ruth did. When the going got tough, she got going…right back to where she came from.

Ruth, however, was a completely different woman. She saw the trials of her mother-in-law. She saw her heartache. She saw her pain and discouragement. She worried about how Naomi would make it back to Bethlehem, given the state of mind that she was in. She had a love for Naomi that only God could place within her, a love that sought what was best for Naomi. It was a love that put her first. It was a love that was willing to go as far as necessary to bring Naomi to the place that she needed to be. It was a love that said, "I will not allow you to do this alone! I will not allow you to face these hardships on your own! I understand what you are going through, and I will be to you more than just another shoulder to cry on. I will walk this long dusty road beside you! I will be a person who is there for you when you fall, and I will help pick you up when you do. I will change my way of life if it somehow benefits you."

You see, the very name Ruth means "friendly." What a true friend she turned out to be! A friend that Naomi could rely on. The mercy of God in Moab had a name. Her name was Ruth!

4

RETURNING HOME

So they both went until they came to Bethlehem. And when they had come to Bethlehem, all the city was stirred because of them, and the women said, "Is this Naomi?" She said to them, "Do not call me Naomi; call me Mara (bitter), for the Almighty has dealt very bitterly with me. I went out full, but the Lord has brought me back empty. Why do you call me Naomi, since the Lord has witnessed against me and the Almighty has afflicted me?"
—Ruth 1:19–21

NOW NAOMI AND RUTH WERE returning to Bethlehem. The entire city noticed her returning home, but something was not right with Naomi. She stopped being the pleasant woman God had called her to be.

The women of Bethlehem all came out to greet her. They asked her, "Naomi, is that really you? Is it your face that I'm seeing?"

Naomi's response, I'm sure, sent shock waves throughout Bethlehem. She said, "I am not pleasant anymore! I am bitter! God punished me! It's all His fault that I lost everything! He took that which was dear to my heart! I blame Him for making me into a bitter old woman!"

Oh, how often I see and hear these words from people today! It's all God's fault! How could He? Where is His love? Why did He allow this to happen? It's pointless to serve Him. All I see is pain and heartache around me. If He is Almighty, then why didn't He do something about my problem before it got too big? People haven't really changed, have they? We may live in a different time than Naomi, but it's all still the same human nature.

What Naomi failed to realize initially was that God didn't tell her to leave the house of bread. She and her husband did that all by themselves. God didn't tell them to give their sons names that cursed their futures. Naomi and Elimelech did that all by themselves too. God didn't create the negative atmosphere around them. They did that one all by themselves too.

How easy it is for us to blame God when we make decisions that are outside of His boundaries of blessing. More often than not, Christians fail to realize this fact until the Holy Spirit breaks through all of the bitterness, and reveals this to them. We at times fail to see this fact even in our everyday lives. For example when you see a speed limit sign say that you can only go 45 mph, it's not because the city is trying to slow your progress or trying to make you late somewhere. It's because the city knows that if you go any higher than the speed they listed, your chances at a fatal accident increases. If a person speeds and crashes, it's not the cities fault. It's that person's fault for leaving the boundaries of safety. So it is with God. When a person makes a willful decision to leave a place of God's blessing, he risks the consequences of his decision.

God didn't take everything away from Naomi. Naomi left God's place of blessing.

> *I will call heaven and earth to witness against you today, that I have set before you life and death, blessing and curse. Therefore choose life, that you and your offspring may live.* (Deuteronomy 30:19)

This scripture says that God placed before us life and death, blessing and curse. It's up to us to decide the right way for not only us but also for our offspring. This scripture was well known at the time of Naomi. God didn't make her bitter. He gave her and her family a choice. However, even though she left that place of blessing, God still loved her and made a provision for her through Ruth. See, Naomi needed to return to the house of bread for her to be reminded of the fact that she was never called to be bitter. God did not give her that name. Her parents didn't give her that name. She gave herself that title. She, like her husband Elimelech, forgot her identity in God.

Can you see how easy it is for us to forget who God has called us to be? We periodically go through moments when we seem to forget who we are in Christ Jesus. This is why it is very important for us to be willing to come back to the house of bread. It is only there that we can remember who we were called to be. It is only in the presence of the Bread of Life that we remember the name He calls us by.

If you are experiencing that same sort of bitterness that Naomi experienced, if you feel like you are not the same person you used to be when you first believed, then maybe it is time to return to the house of bread and be reminded of who God has called you to be in Christ Jesus. God will never leave you in a place of bitterness! He loves you too much! Even if you have made some wrong decisions in life, He still provides a way out. Just like He did for Naomi, He will place a Ruth in your life to bring you to a place where you need to be.

> *Behold, it was for my welfare that I had great bitterness; but in love you have delivered my life from the pit of destruction, for you have cast all my sins behind your back.* (Isaiah 38:17)

What a beautiful scripture this is! *In Your love, You delivered my life. You cast all my sins behind Your back. In other words, in spite of my poor decisions that led me to this place, You have provided a way out because you love me.* This is the true character of God. He is so loving, that He is willing to forget what we've done wrong in order to save our lives.

This is what Naomi experienced through Ruth. When Naomi was returning to Bethlehem, Ruth was right behind her, encouraging her the whole way. Even when they arrived at Bethlehem, Naomi was bitter. It was Ruth who was going out to the fields to find grain for them to make bread to eat.

The return home wasn't an easy one, but it was necessary. I'm sure the road back to Bethlehem was not an easy road to travel. Try to place yourself there at that time. It was roughly about a fifty-mile journey from Moab to Bethlehem. On foot, it would have taken around a week to complete the trip. It was probably hot walking on the road. It was dusty, rocky, and probably hard. During the walk, you would have to stop and find water to drink if you didn't carry enough with you in your waterpot. Maybe a donkey was carrying Naomi's belongings and waterpots. However, in spite of how hard the journey was, Naomi had Ruth right beside her as she went.

Oh, how important it is that we have others around us to encourage us in our walk with Christ! We must remember that we are never alone. Even when we know that we made a wrong decision in life, we have to keep in mind that God always has a way out. If we are willing to receive it, He will send help our way to walk beside us on our journey back to Him. Making a decision to return to the place that we know we belong is not an easy one. However, when we make that decision, we must be willing to walk the road back to Bethlehem no matter how hard it may seem at times. When we do so, God will send the right people our way to help us get back to Bethlehem.

> *Two are better than one, because they have a good reward for their toil. For if they fall, one will lift up the other. But woe to the one who falls and has not another to lift him up!* (Ecclesiastes 4:9–10)

Whenever we walk on the road back to Bethlehem or back to the place that we were called to be, we can always be sure that God will place a Ruth right beside us. Even when Jesus sent out His disciples, He made sure that they traveled by twos. We cannot do it alone. This is why God said that it was not good for man to be alone when He created Adam.

What was the thought process of Naomi at that time? What must have been going through her head? Were her thoughts like, *What am I going to do when I get back? How will I find bread to eat again? What if the people of Bethlehem don't receive me? Will my old house still be available? Are there any relatives left in Bethlehem? How do I tell everyone that my husband and sons are dead? Will they look at me any differently now that I returned from Moab?* I'm sure that some of these thoughts may have been going through her head. Perhaps she was contemplating how she was going to get back on her feet. Only now she had a daughter-in-law who refuses to take no for an answer. Thank God for Ruth's stubbornness! She refused to allow Naomi to walk alone and bear this burden by herself.

Whatever the case may have been, Naomi was now arriving at Bethlehem. Oh, the memories that must have come back to her! Perhaps she saw some places or things that reminded her of her past happiness in life, things that reminded her of her sons and husband. Then a sudden feeling of emptiness must have overtaken her. But right when she might have felt that, there was Ruth to encourage her and help her to press on.

But if you return to me and keep my commandments and do them, though those of you who have been scattered were in the most remote part of the heavens, I will gather them from there and will bring them to the place where I have chosen to cause My name to dwell. (Nehemiah 1:9)

As they arrive in Bethlehem, the whole town stirred over her arrival. She must have felt a little overwhelmed. She might not have expected the house of bread to have missed her presence so much. Yet they greet her with joy! Even though she called herself bitter, they still know her by the name that God called her by.

Can I just tell you that even when you mess up in life, feel unworthy, and even feel like you haven't lived up to the name God called you by, He never changes His mind about you! Like Naomi experienced, you will also find out that the house of bread misses fellowship with you!

Even though Naomi was in a place of bitterness while in Moab, as soon as she made a decision to return to the house of bread, God turned her into an evangelist. Once she said that she was going back to the house of bread, Ruth decided to go with her. Do you remember what Ruth said to Naomi? "Your people shall be my people, and your God shall be my God." Wow! Even though Naomi just decided to return to where she needed to be, God made her an evangelist! He saw her heart, and He chose to use her life for His glory in order to save a young woman from Moab! Ruth found mercy through the Lord God of Israel.

She then became an instrument of mercy for the woman who led her to the Lord.

Never underestimate the power of God in your life! As soon as you decide to come back to the house of bread, God begins to work again in your life! This is what happens to anyone who is willing to walk away from the house of death and return to a place that I like to call home, the house of bread—or better known as Bethlehem.

Naomi had now returned to the house of bread. She was home again.

5

A KINSMAN REDEEMER

*Now Naomi had a kinsman of her husband, a man
of great wealth, of the family of Elimilech, whose
name was Boaz. And Ruth the Moabitess said to
Naomi, "Please let me go to the field and glean among
the ears of grain after one in whose sight I may find
favor." And she said to her, "Go my daughter."*
—Ruth 2:1–2

AFTER NAOMI RETURNED TO BETHLEHEM with Ruth, she
found out that her deceased husband had a relative in
Bethlehem named Boaz. He was a very wealthy man. Ruth
decided to ask Naomi if she could begin gleaning from his
field in order for them to have bread.

It is possible that Naomi knew who Boaz was but perhaps they were never really close. After all, she had been
married to his relative, Elimilech. However, to what extent
she was acquainted with Boaz isn't clear. All the Bible tells
us is that he was a kinsman, another word for a relative.
However, I would imagine that he was very important to
the town of Bethlehem because he was very well known as a
wealthy person. It is possible that his fields were the source

of bread for Bethlehem. It is possible that Bethlehem relied upon his grain to make bread for Israel. Whatever the case might have been, he was harvesting the grain to make bread at the time of Naomi's return to Bethlehem.

If they were harvesting the barley grain during the time of Naomi's return, it had to be in the spring. You see, in ancient Israel, the barley and wheat crops were planted in the fall and harvested in the spring. It would have been between March or April by our calendar. On the Jewish calendar, it was the month of Nisan. This is very important to recognize because of the spiritual significance of this time. This time period, interestingly enough, is around the same time as Passover. Passover is on the fifteenth day of the month of Nisan. According to the laws of Israel, no one could eat of the grain of the barley harvest until the first fruits of the harvest were cut on the day before Passover and brought as a grain offering on the second day of the festival. Only then could a person enjoy the fruits of the grain that was harvested.

If Ruth was gleaning from the fields, then it must have been around the time in which the firstfruits had already been offered for Passover. Now she is gathering grain to feed Naomi and herself from the field of Boaz, in the house of bread, on the festival of Passover, through the goodness of a kinsman redeemer! She finds favor in the eyes of this redeemer! Ruth was a type of mercy and friendship to Naomi. Now mercy found favor in the eyes of a redeemer in the house of bread during a time of Passover.

What a beautiful picture of Jesus Christ!!! He meets them in the house of bread during a time of redemption.

Only He can restore to them everything that was lost! The Lamb has been sacrificed, the firstfruits have been offered, the fields are ripe with plenty of bread, and the redeemer waits for them to come to Him so that He can redeem their lives! There is no judgment, no condemnation, and no "I told you so." All that there is *is* His unfailing love and mercy!

They returned to Bethlehem to find a kinsman redeemer. They returned to Bethlehem at a time when the redeemer prepared a field for them to find grain. They found a redeemer who is willing to redeem them out of their sad state. It is said that he was a very wealthy person so he had the ability to redeem their lives. He had the ability to restore to them all that which was lost through the mistakes of Naomi and Elimelech. He did so with such love and tenderness! He saw Ruth and made a way for her to eat plenty of bread in a time of harvest. He saw that she was caring for Naomi. He chose to not only meet her needs, but he also extended an invitation to her to sit with him at his table and have fellowship with him.

Oh, how I see Jesus all over this story! Oh how I see His unfailing love toward His people! You see, just as Boaz made a way for Ruth to find bread and then invited her to sit and dine with him at his table, Jesus also extends that same invitation to you and me. He desires for us to come to Him in the house of bread where He has already made provision for us. He asks us to come and dine with Him. He desires fellowship with us!

Boaz invited Ruth to eat with him and then commanded his servants to drop grain for her to glean.

When she arose to glean, Boaz commanded his servants, saying, "Let her glean even among the sheaves, and do not insult her. Also you shall purposely pull out for her some grain from the bundles and leave it that she may glean, and do not rebuke her."
(Ruth 2:15–16)

Here we see the kindness of this man. He was well known, he was wealthy, he was busy, and yet he took notice of a foreign woman in his field gathering grain. He invited her to eat with him and found out that she was with his relative Naomi. He then began to show kindness toward her and personally saw to it that she was fed. He concerned himself with their problems. He reached down to their state and began to lift them out of their problems.

There are no words of condemnation. There are no words of self-righteousness. There is no rebuke to Naomi for leaving with her husband to Moab. There is no just punishment for their decisions. All there is *is* love, mercy, and a second chance at life in Bethlehem.

Can you imagine Noemi's shock when Ruth brought back home several sheaves of grain? Can you imagine what she must have felt like when Ruth told her that Boaz showed kindness to them? As soon as Naomi found out, she changed from a bitter person to a person who was broken by the love of a redeemer in Bethlehem. Her bitterness turned into hope. Her past was being swallowed up by her future in Bethlehem. She started to get excited for Ruth! She told her to go and ask him to redeem them as a relative redeemer.

> *Then Naomi her mother-in-law said to her, "My daughter, shall I not seek security for you, that it may be well with you? Now is not Boaz our kinsman, with whose maids you were? Behold, he threshes barley at the threshing floor tonight. Wash yourself therefore and anoint yourself and put on your best clothes and go down to the threshing floor."*
> (Ruth 3:1–3)

Ruth did exactly what Naomi said. Boaz was a little shocked at how she laid at his feet, seeking a covering of redemption for her and Naomi. She asked him to redeem her. She came into his presence in the house of bread where he was preparing the grain, and she laid at his feet, seeking redemption from him.

I see Jesus all over this story! I see His mercy and redemption in this passage of scripture. It reminds me of another passage of scripture:

> *But she has washed my feet with her tears and dried them with her hair. You didn't greet me with a kiss, but from the time I came in, she has not stopped kissing my feet. You didn't pour olive oil on my head, but she has poured expensive perfume on my feet. So*

I tell you that all of her sins are forgiven, and that is why she has shown great love. (Luke 7:44–47)

You see, as soon as Naomi made a decision to return to the house of bread, God made a decision to show her mercy. She returned to the house of bread to find a redeemer during the time of Passover who showed her love and met her hunger with his bread. She found someone who was willing and able to redeem her life from the mistakes of the past.

This is what Bethlehem is. It is a house of bread. It is a place of life. It is a place in which we have a Redeemer who is willing to help us, if we would only come to Him. This is a place that has bread for the Passover. This is a place that has a Redeemer who has the ability to redeem anyone willing to ask Him. This is a place that feeds the hungry soul. This is a place that shows mercy when there should be justice. There is a Redeemer in the house of bread! He is willing to feed you if you would be willing to just come to Him. He is willing to fellowship with you if you are will-ing to enter His field. He is willing to spread His covering over you and redeem you if you would humble yourself before Him and fall at His feet. That is the place that you can truly find rest from your weary journey. That is the place where you can find His peace, alone in His presence. This is a place that already had the Passover sacrifice for your redemption. This is a place that extends the hand of God's favor to you not based upon your works, not based upon what you have done, but rather based upon what was already accomplished for you by your own kinsman redeemer.

See, you and I have a kinsman redeemer. We have someone who is familiar with our struggles. We have someone who has lived among us and has faced all of the temptations we have faced. We have a Redeemer who is both the Son of Man and the Son of God. He has already done all that needed to be done for you. He already planted the grain for you to eat of the *bread of life*. He already brought forth the firstfruits of His offering for the Passover sacrifice for your sins. He already prepared the waterpot for you to fellowship with Him and drink of the *water of life*. He already prepared the covering of grace for you to hide under. He already paid the price for you to find peace in his house. He already made a way for you to once again experience life though Him. All you have to do is turn around and walk back to Bethlehem.

It is very difficult for a Christian to understand at times that his or her own salvation does not depend upon them. Whenever we make the same dangerous decision to do what Elimelech did, we find ourselves in a state of spiritual hunger and death. Elimelech thought that his life and the lives of his family depended upon him. He thought that he could feed his family and provide them bread in his own strength. He couldn't do that for them. He couldn't even do that for himself. He was incapable of providing the bread necessary for even his own sustenance.

This is what happens when we fail to realize that the house of bread has a kinsman redeemer who has already done it all for us. We spiritually drift from the place that we are supposed to be. If we want to find life in the house of bread, then we must first realize that the provision for the bread has already been made for us. We must realize that we live by faith, not by feeling. Our salvation, our justification, our sanctification, and our very life doesn't depend upon us. It depends upon the one who has already made provision for us in the house of bread. It depends upon the one who is waiting for us to come to him so that He can redeem our broken lives. There is a kinsman redeemer in the house of bread. His name is Jesus Christ!

6

A Restorer of Life

When she came to her mother-in-law, she said, "How did it go, my daughter?" And she told her all that the man had done for her. She said, "These six measures of barley he gave to me, for he said, 'Do not go to your mother-in-law empty-handed.'" Then she said, "Wait, my daughter, until you know how the matter turns out; for the man will not rest until he has settled it today."
—Ruth 3:16–18

ONCE NAOMI AND RUTH FOUND out that they have a kinsman redeemer, they placed their entire trust in him. They understood that only he could redeem them and restore everything that was lost. After Ruth went to Boaz, she had to wait alongside Naomi for his act of redemption to be completed. He gave Ruth six measures of barley and sent her to feed Naomi. He worked behind the scenes, redeeming and restoring that which was lost.

He went to the gate of the city to do business. He met another relative there who also had a legal right to redeem what was once Elimelech's. However, this relative turned down that offer because the stipulations of redemption were not to his liking. You see, the stipulation for redeeming Naomi and Ruth was that whoever redeems them would have to also marry Ruth in order for their family line to continue. This was the price that Boaz was willing to pay in order to redeem Ruth and Naomi. He was willing to not only feed them but also raise up a family line through them. You see, this kinsman redeemer was so loving that he was willing to raise up a family line for those who left the house of bread. He was not willing to allow Elimelech's name to be cut off from the earth. He was not willing to allow his family line to perish. He knew that in redeeming Naomi and Ruth, he would be continuing in the line of Elimelech. He was not ashamed of being the one who was used to preserve the family line of Elimelech. Even though Elimelech once left the house of bread, lived in a moment of unbelief, and doubted the provision of God, the redeemer was still willing to preserve his family line! He was willing to raise a seed in the house of Elimelech that would dwell every day in the house of bread and eat continually at his table of provision. He was willing to take them under his wing and care for them.

> Then Boaz said to all the elders and all the people, "You are my witnesses today that I bought from the hand of Naomi all that belonged to Elimelech and all that belonged to Chilion and Mahlon. Moreover, I have acquired Ruth the Moabitess, the widow of Mahlon, to be my wife in order to raise up the name of the deceased on his inheritance,

*so that the name of the deceased will not be
cut off from his brothers or from the court of
his birthplace; you are my witnesses today."*
(Ruth 4:9–10)

Here is a picture of not only redemption but also total restoration. Boaz is publicly announcing that he is willing to redeem this family in such a way that they would never be cut off from the house of bread. He believes in selfless, sacrificial redemption, a sort of redemption that restores everything that was once lost.

He says, "I will redeem you in such a way that you will have children, you will have a future and a hope."

*"For I know the plans I have for you,"
declares the Lord, "plans to prosper you and
not to harm you, to give you hope and a
future." (Jeremiah 29:11)*

You will not be limited by your past. You will not even remember the former things. All things will become new. His type of redemption is a total redemption. It's a redemption that gives a person a renewed joy and a new strength. It's a redemption that restores a person's life and brings that person to a place of complete peace.

Boaz covered Ruth. Ruth came to Boaz by night and asked him to cover her:

*It happened in the middle of the night
that the man was startled and bent forward;*

and behold, a woman was lying at his feet. He said, "Who are you?" And she answered, "I am Ruth your maid. So spread your covering over your maid, for you are a close relative." (Ruth 3:8–9)

Ruth came to Boaz and asked him to cover her under his covering. She understood that the only place she can find redemption is under the covering that he provided her.

This is the same thing that Jesus does for all of us when we make the decision to come to Him in the house of bread. He covers us with His redemptive covering. That redemptive covering is His own blood.

In Him we have redemption through His blood, the forgiveness of our sins, according to the riches of His grace. (Ephesians 1:7)

This is the covering that Jesus Christ spreads out for us, His people. The covering for our sins is the precious blood of Jesus Christ. When we make the decision to come to Him and to ask for His covering over us, we will find what Ruth found in Boaz—peace. It is peace that is above human understanding, which gives us rest at the feet of the redeemer, and promises us a future and a hope. This is what God says to His people, "I will give you hope and a future. Not because you deserve it. Not because you earned it. Not because you are perfect. But because I am good to you." God will not allow us to be cut off from the earth or forgotten due to our past. He is not afraid to associate with sinners. He is not afraid to redeem our lives in such a way that we begin to bear fruit once more.

This is what happened with Naomi. She learned that God is a God of mercy and love. She learned that she could pick up where she left off and continue to dwell in the house of bread. All she had to do was make a decision to return, and God would prepare for her a way of redemption. Naomi learned that God wasn't the one who made her bitter, but He was the one who restored to her through a kinsman redeemer. This reminds me of another passage of scripture:

> *I will restore to you the years that the locusts have eaten, the cankerworm, and the caterpillar, and the palmerworm.* (Joel 2:25)

This is the Lord's promise to His people. He will restore all that was lost at the hands of the enemy or through your own foolish decisions if you would be willing to just come to Him in the house of bread.

Boaz redeemed all that belonged to Elimelech. His wife, his daughter-in-law, his land, his house, and his very name was redeemed through Boaz. This is what a redeemer does. He redeems at one hundred percent. He doesn't just redeem a part of something. He redeems all of it. Everything is restored through him. Boaz knew that everything that once belonged to Elimelech must be redeemed. He was willing to pay the price necessary in order to ensure total redemption.

How many Christians go through their Christian lives with a mentality of partial redemption? How many Christians say that they believe in the redemption that they have obtained through Christ, but they act as if He only partially redeemed them. They only believe in the partial promise of redemption. They only live as if they have been partially redeemed. How many Christians believe that Christ redeemed their souls yet they don't believe in the healing that they also obtained through his wounds? How many believe that they have obtained salvation yet doubt that they have also obtained complete deliverance?

If Jesus is your redeemer, then you must realize that He redeemed not only your soul but also your body, your life, your future, and everything that is associated with you personally. You cannot limit the terms of His redemption for you. He knew that the price He paid was more than enough to bring about total redemption within you. This is what Boaz did for Naomi and Ruth. He brought about total redemption.

Something beautiful happens when redemption is made for a person. Something happens as a direct result of redemption. That something is called fruit. It's called becoming fruitful in the house of bread through a kinsman redeemer. You see, when a person is redeemed, they show that they are redeemed through bearing fruit. It's called the fruit of the redeemer. It is his life being brought forth in you. It is his seed that grows within you. It is his banner of protection that ensures your redemption. It is his redemption that restores your life. The kinsman redeemer is also the restorer of life. Just as Boaz was the restorer of life for Naomi and Ruth, so is Jesus Christ our Redeemer and the Restorer of life for all who are willing to come to Him in the house of bread and find redemption at His feet and under His covering. Boaz was a restorer of life, but he was also a type and shadow of the ultimate redeemer and restorer of life, Jesus Christ.

7

A FRUITFUL WOMB

So Boaz took Ruth, and she became his wife,
and he went into her. And the Lord enabled her
to conceive, and she gave birth to a son.

—Ruth 4:13

NOW WE COME TO A beautiful part of this story. It is a part of renewed life and a fruitful womb. It's a moment when the past is swallowed up by the victory of redemption.

Can you imagine the joy that Naomi was feeling? Can you imagine how happy she is to see the birth of her grandchild? Boaz placed within Ruth the future of their family, the future of their names, and the future of their lives. He raised up a seed that was once lost due to sin and unbelief. He restored what was once thought to have perished in Moab. He redeemed that which seemed completely hopeless. The joy that must have been on Naomi's face caused her to suddenly forget the pain of the past. It made her to look forward to the future. She was able to hold in her arms the promise of life that she thought died in Moab. She must have felt totally overwhelmed by her emotions! She probably cried tears of joy as she greeted her grandson who would carry on the name of her children. The restorer of life, the redeemer of the hopeless, and the mercy of the loving Boaz brought to life all that was once lost!

This is exactly what Jesus does for us. He places within us the seal of our redemption, His Holy Spirit. By doing so, we begin to realize that we have a future because of Him. We start to grab a hold of the promises of God for us. We start to feel the reality of His presence inside us. This is what the apostle Paul talked about, the seal of the promise of God placed within us.

> *In Him you also, when you heard the word of truth, the gospel of your salvation, and believed in him, were sealed with the promised Holy Spirit, who is the guarantee of our inheritance until we acquire possession of it, to the praise of His glory.* (Ephesians 1:13–14)

This is what redemption truly looks like, taking that which was lost and causing it to bear fruit. The fruitless womb of Ruth became a fruitful womb through Boaz. Through the redeemer, a promise was placed within her. That promise became reality when a son was born to her. At the time of the child's birth, the entire village came to witness the fruit of the kinsman redeemer become a reality. They were excited and overjoyed!

The women of the town began to bless Naomi. They began to speak life into her. They began to proclaim over her all of the promises of her forefathers. They reminded her that her name was not bitter! The name that she gave herself was not who she was, thanks to the love of her kinsman redeemer! She was reminded of the name that her father once gave her.

Naomi (pleasant), the one who was kind enough to restore her life rather than condemn her mistakes, helped her to once again realize that she had been called by a different name a long time ago. Her circumstances tried to erase the name given to her, but her circumstances couldn't overpower the love of a redeemer. It couldn't overcome the one who was willing to restore her life.

> *Then the women said to Naomi, "Blessed is the Lord who has not left you without a redeemer today, and may his name be famous in Israel. May he also be to you a restorer of life and a sustainer of your old age; for your daughter-in-law, who loves you and is better to you than seven sons, has given birth to him."* (Ruth 4:14–15)

Boaz means "strength is within him." The kinsman redeemer had the strength within himself to redeem for Naomi and Ruth that which was lost. They didn't have to rely upon their own strength to redeem or to fix that which was lost. They didn't have to try to do it all on their own. They didn't have to try to take matters into their own hands in order to restore everything that seemed forever lost.

It is the same way for you and me. We don't have to try to redeem our own lives through our own strength. We don't have to try to fix all of our mistakes on our own. We don't have to try to restore all that was lost due to our foolish decisions. Our redemption cannot happen with our own strength. We do not have the strength within ourselves to do any of this. That is why we have a wonderful Redeemer who has the strength within Himself to redeem and restore all that which was broken or lost.

If we would be just willing to come to Him and ask, He is faithful to do this for us. This is what happens when we make the decision to return to the house of bread, no matter the past mistakes that we have made in life. Whenever we choose to return to the house of bread, we find that all is not lost. We discover that the giver of life places His seed within us. He brings forth life out of us, and through that life, He restores all that we thought was once lost. He shows us that all is not lost if we would just allow Him to place within us His Holy Spirit. All is not lost if we would just allow Him to place His Son within us.

The women of Bethlehem living around Naomi gave the child a name. Isn't that interesting? Naomi didn't name the boy. Ruth didn't name the boy. Boaz didn't name the boy. The people living around them named him. Those who daily surrounded Naomi and Ruth gave the boy a name.

This is a type and shadow of what happens to us when we allow ourselves to be filled with the presence of God, then we begin to bear fruit for His kingdom. Those surrounding us on a daily basis start to give that fruit a name. They see God at work within us, and they recognize all that He begins to bring forth in our lives.

The women of Bethlehem give the baby a beautiful name. They called him Obed, which means "servant." A servant is born to them who will work among them and begin to restore all that was lost through his father. This servant works through the strength of his father. He takes all that belongs to his father and gives it to them. He makes his father's inheritance, the inheritance of Naomi and Ruth. This redeemer works to restore the fortunes of Naomi and Ruth. This child became a servant to them so that they might become the inheritance of his father. Sound familiar? Does this not remind you of someone? His father is the strength, but he is the servant. He works in his father's fields, bringing in the harvest so that those redeemed by his father might have the bread of life continually. As he grows, he becomes the servant of his father's house, helping to redeem, through the will of his father and through his father's strength, the family of Elimelech, a family that he also identifies with because he was born through them and is also their son.

Once again, we see Jesus Christ, a Son born to the children of men by the will and strength of His Father to help redeem a lost world that His Father chose to save through Him. He was also a servant to both His Father and to men. One that would be the provider of the bread of life for all those who live in His Father's house, the house of bread.

For God so loved the world, that He gave
His one and only Son, that whoever would
believe in Him would not perish, but have
everlasting life. For God did not send His

Son into the world to condemn the world,
but that the world through Him might be
saved. (John 3:16–17)

Finally, in the last chapter of the book of Ruth, it lists the genealogy of David. King David came through Ruth. Jesus came through Ruth. God is never ashamed to be identified with you when you make the decision to come to the house of bread to let Him redeem your life. The genealogy was placed there for us to study so that we might also see a hidden message within it. God never places something in the Bible for no reason. Allow me to try to reveal this meaning to you today. There are several names placed here. We will take them in order one by one and try to paint a picture of redemption.

The first name listed at the end of Ruth chapter 4 is Perez whose name means "breakout, or breakthrough."

The next name is Hezron. His name means "encloser" or "enclosure." Then there is the name Aram, which means "elevated." Next is Amminadab whose name means "my kinsman are noble" or "kindred of the prince." Then we see the name Nahshon. His name means "one that foretells." Now we come to the name Salmon (not the fish). His name means "peace, perfect, and he who rewards." Now we come to the name of the kinsman redeemer, Boaz. His name, as we already read, means "strength is within him." Now the name of his son Obed, who was born to him through Ruth, means "servant." Obed had a son. His son's name was Jesse. The name Jesse means a "gift." Finally, Jesse's son David means "beloved."

So if we were to put all these names together, we would form a picture of redemption. Let's try that. Break out of the enclosure that is elevated. The kindred of the prince foretells perfect peace, his reward. His strength is within the servant, a gift to the beloved. What a wonderful foreshadow of the coming of the Messiah! Even the book of Ruth reveals the redemptive plan of God for His people!

Just as Naomi and Ruth found restoration for the house of Elimelech through Boaz, may you too find this same restoration for your own life through the eternal Redeemer, Jesus Christ. All you have to do go back to the place where you belong at the house of bread, just like what Naomi and Ruth did.

I hope that this book was an encouragement to you and that you would find redemption in the One who came to Bethlehem two thousand years ago so that you too might find hope and a future in what He already accomplished for us on a cross. Remember, your Redeemer loves you!